Cornerstones of Freedom

The Story of

THE BURNING OF WASHINGTON

By R. Conrad Stein

Illustrated by Richard Wahl

 CHILDRENS PRESS ™
CHICAGO

Library of Congress Cataloging in Publication Data

Stein, R. Conrad.
  The story of the burning of Washington.

  (Cornerstones of freedom)
  Summary: Describes the events of the British
invasion and burning of Washington, D.C. in 1814.
    1. Washington, (D.C.) — History — Capture by the
British, 1814 — Juvenile literature. [1. Washington
(D.C.) — History — Capture by the British, 1814.
    2. United States — History — War of 1812] I. Wahl,
Richard, 1939-   ill. II. Title. III. Series.
E356.W3S83   1984   975.3'02   84-12124
  ISBN 0-516-04678-0   AACR2

The sun rose blazingly hot over Benedict, Maryland, on the morning of August 20, 1814. A dozen warships bristling with guns drifted lazily before the tiny town's waterfront. Small boats carrying troops inched close to the beach. Sweating and swearing in the heat, some forty-five hundred British soldiers climbed down ramps and splashed ashore. Although the men were invading hostile ground, not one shot was fired at them. The British landing had caught the Americans completely by surprise.

On the high ground, the troops, clad in red jackets and carrying heavy packs, formed ranks. With fifes playing and drums beating, the British redcoats marched off smartly, as if on a parade ground.

Even before the first redcoat stepped ashore, riders galloped their horses out of Benedict to spread the alarm that the British had landed. For more than a year, British warships had patrolled the coast, but these were the first enemy soldiers this sleepy Maryland community had seen. Some people wondered where the redcoats were heading, but the military scouts had no doubts. They carried messages to their commanders reading: "The enemy is in full march to Washington."

Today Washington, D.C. is a citadel of power and a city of rare beauty. But in 1814 it was a capital with no past to speak of, and not much in the way of a present. About eight thousand people lived in Washington at the time of the British invasion. Twenty years earlier the city did not even exist. The site was a dreary swamp on the banks of the Potomac River. Congress declared Washington to be its new Federal City in 1791, but not until 1800 did the American government officially move there from Philadelphia. In 1814, Washington had an air of unfinished emptiness, and most Americans considered it just another country town and a capital in name only.

Surprisingly, Washingtonians seemed only mildly

disturbed when they learned that a British army was marching toward their city. Their leaders assured them that a militia of from eight thousand to ten thousand men could be assembled within a few hours' notice to defend the capital. Washington's leading newspaper, the *National Intelligencer*, claimed, "We feel assured that the number and bravery of our men will afford complete protection to the city." Equally confident was a leading Washington society figure named Mrs. Margaret Bayard Smith. She wrote, "Our troops were eager for an attack, and such was the cheerful alacrity displayed that a universal confidence reigned among [Washington's] citizens and people."

But not everyone in Washington was so certain of the city's invincibility. In the White House, President James Madison conferred with Secretary of State James Monroe. (At that time the White House was called the President's House, and portions of it were still being built. Many of its rooms smelled of wet cement.) During their meeting, Monroe warned the president that the militia defending the capital consisted mainly of untrained farm boys. The secretary wondered how well they would fight against disciplined British regulars. At the end of their conference, Monroe saddled his horse and rode out to get a firsthand view of the American troops. President Madison paced the hallway. Finally he scratched out a letter to his wife, advising her to be prepared to evacuate the White House "at a moment's warning."

The British force hiked north over the Maryland countryside so casually that an observer would have guessed the men were on peacetime maneuvers. At one point, an advance patrol discovered two Americans carrying muskets with bayonets attached. They were probably members of the militia, but the two told the redcoats they were merely out hunting rabbits.

Meanwhile, American General William Winder rode madly from village to village trying to assemble his militia. Winder was a prominent Baltimore lawyer who had received a high commission in the infantry two years earlier. So far his military career was a disaster. In his only previous engagement, Winder had been captured by the British during a skirmish in Canada. The British had released him as part of a prisoner exchange. Now charged with the defense of Washington, Winder had failed to dig trenches or emplace cannons at the city's ap-

proaches. And on the eve of battle he could not even find his troops.

For almost three days Winder hurried about the countryside while the British marched undisturbed. By the time the general assembled a sufficient number of troops, the British column had reached Bladensburg, Maryland, just five miles from Washington. At Bladensburg, a bridge spanned a shallow stream. A crucial battle in the War of 1812 was about to begin.

In its long history, the American army has scored many brilliant victories, but the Battle of Bladensburg stands as a stain on the country's military record. At Bladensburg, the redcoats routed a poorly led and badly frightened American force.

The British began the battle with a two-pronged attack on the bridge. One unit of redcoats assaulted the bridge directly, while another splashed through the shallow water and stormed the opposite bank. Almost seven thousand American militiamen had formed ranks at the riverfront to stop the British advance. But they were a ragtag bunch, hastily assembled and poorly trained. Looking at the American defenders, one British officer wrote, "A few companies only. . .presented some appearance of regular troops. The rest seemed country people who would have been more appropriately employed attending to their agricultural occupations than standing with muskets in their hands on a bare hill."

As the British approached the bridge, the American militia fired their muskets. Their first volley came from far too long a range; the wild shots revealed the soldiers' inexperience. The Americans reloaded and fired again. This time a dozen British soldiers fell. Still, the tough, disciplined redcoats

pushed forward. From a distant hill, a British squadron launched newly designed rockets at the American ranks. The rockets did little damage, but the strange fire-tailed missiles with their whooshing sounds struck terror in the hearts of the farm boys who made up the militia.

The American defenders were further weakened by chaotic leadership. The battle was fought just one hour's ride from the Capitol. Consequently, scores of powerful Washingtonians—congressmen and cabinet ministers—galloped to Bladensburg to help defend Washington. Once on the battleground, the politicians began acting as if they were army commanders and started ordering the troops about. Secretary of State James Monroe moved lines of militiamen here and there, confusing the already bewildered American soldiers. Another self-proclaimed officer was a Georgetown lawyer, Francis Scott Key. He later won lasting fame in American history, but as a combat officer he, too, was a dismal failure.

A strong army commander would have banished the politicians-turned-generals, but General Winder was not the man for the task. Hours before the battle, he wrote, "I am but a nominal commander. The [others] have interfered with my intended operations, and I greatly fear the success of the day." One corporal in the American ranks claimed that the only order he heard Winder issue was "When you retreat, take notice you must retreat by the Georgetown Road."

The screaming rockets and the relentless British foot soldiers proved too formidable a force for the disorganized Americans. At first, small units fell back. Then whole companies bolted and ran. The battle became a rout. Only one group of armed sailors and marines under a captain named Barney put up a determined fight, but they alone could not stop the British.

After the redcoats swept over the river, a forward unit climbed a hill at the far end of Bladensburg. Below they saw the city of Washington lying unprotected by American troops. A major prize in the War of 1812 would soon go to the British.

The War of 1812 is sometimes called America's second War of Independence. Many of the country's most powerful leaders (including the president himself) were young men in 1776, and had helped win independence from the British. America entered

this second War of Independence for two major reasons—European interference with American shipping and the influence of a group of feisty frontier congressmen.

In the first decade of the 1800s, Great Britain was locked in a life-and-death struggle with France. Britain needed sailors and stopped American ships on the high seas to impress (seize) American seamen, who were forced to work on British ships. France needed ships and captured American merchant vessels for use in the French navy. One American congressman wrote, "The devil himself could not tell which government, England or France, is the most wicked."

In 1810 France, led by Napoleon, agreed to stop interfering with American shipping. In turn, the United States promised to cut off trade with the British. After holding off for a year and a half, the British finally decided they, too, would leave American ships and seamen alone. But two days before the British announcement, the United States Congress declared war on Great Britain. Ironically, had the overseas telegraph or radio existed at the time, the War of 1812 probably would never have been fought.

Pressure from a group of congressmen known as the War Hawks also goaded Congress into declaring war. The War Hawks were led by Henry Clay of Kentucky and John C. Calhoun of South Carolina. Most came from frontier districts in the south and west. The War Hawks believed that the British intended to supply arms to the Indians in order to attack outlying American settlements. Furthermore, the War Hawks hoped the United States would defeat Great Britain and seize Canada, Britain's huge colony to the north.

Early in the war, the United States enjoyed success at sea, but suffered bitter defeats on land. The initial sea battles were fought off the New England coast and in the Great Lakes. The splendid American frigate *Constitution* opened the fighting by sinking a mighty British warship. Later the *Constitution* earned the nickname Old Ironsides because British cannonballs thudded harmlessly off her copper-sheathed sides. On land, however, American attacks on Canada were driven back. One American army unit captured Toronto (then called York), but was quickly driven out of the city. Before they retreated, American troops set fire to a few of Toronto's public buildings. Because the Americans

had left portions of Toronto in flames, the British army sought revenge.

The war took a new direction in 1814 when Napoleon was defeated in Europe. This enabled Great Britain to move powerful armies to the New World. One of those armies, fresh from Europe, defeated the Americans at Bladensburg and now stood poised to march into Washington.

In Washington the mood shifted from one of confidence to panic. Streams of civilians and defeated militiamen choked the streets. One Washingtonian

wrote a letter describing the frenzy in the capital:
"The distress here and in Georgetown is beyond any
description. Women and children running in every
direction. . . .If the force of the enemy is as large as
stated this city will fall. . . .All is confusion as you
may easily imagine. . . .Stages, hacks, carts, or
wagons cannot be procured for love or money. They
are all pressed for the military. I have just returned
from taking a load of children eight miles out of
town, and the whole distance the road was filled
with women and children. Indeed I never saw so

much distress in my life as today. . . .I am fearful that by twelve o'clock tomorrow this city will not be ours."

At the White House, Dolley Madison waited anxiously for her husband, the president, to return. He had ridden off early in the morning to visit the fighting front. To ease the tension of her wait, Mrs. Madison wrote a letter to her sister: "Will you believe it, we have had a battle near Bladensburg, and I am still here within the sound of the cannon! Mr. Madison comes not. May God protect him."

While the president's wife wrote, two dust-covered messengers galloped up to the White House and banged on the front door. One of the messengers cried, "Clear out, clear out! The general has ordered a retreat."

A lesser person, fearing capture by the enemy, would have fled in panic. But Mrs. Madison was a cool, confident woman. She intended to evacuate Washington, but she would leave with dignity and only when she was certain that her house was in order. First, many of Mr. Madison's government papers had to be taken with her. It would be embarrassing for the president's documents to fall into the hands of the British. And, most important of all, she was determined to protect what she believed to be the prized possession in the White House—the marvelous portrait of George Washington that hung in the large drawing room.

The portrait showed the first president standing proudly with his sword at his side. It had been painted by Gilbert Stuart, one of America's most accomplished artists. Dolley Madison told her servants to take the painting down, box it up, and put it in the wagon waiting to take her to safety. The servants discovered that the frame was bolted to the wall. So Mrs. Madison ordered them to break the frame. Just before she fled the White House, the First Lady finished her letter: "[I placed] the precious portrait in the hands of some gentlemen from New York for safekeeping. And now, dear sister, I must leave this house, or the army will make me a prisoner in it. . . .When I shall again write you or where I shall be tomorrow, I cannot tell!!"

A half hour after Mrs. Madison's wagon carried her away, the president and Attorney General Richard Rush rode up to the White House. They rested for an hour, then decided they, too, must leave Washington. No doubt the president's spirits were devastated upon leaving his capital to the

enemy. But with the British at the city's gates he was as powerless to defend the capital as any other citizen. According to one witness, Mr. Madison "cooly mounted his horse" and rode off with his party to the Potomac River crossing.

At 6:00 P.M. on August 24, 1814, the British entered Washington, D.C. They found the city streets deserted. Those Washingtonians who had not escaped huddled in their homes.

Naval admiral Sir George Cockburn served as overall commander of the British troops. Witnesses said he took a fiendish delight in igniting some of the capital's most important buildings. The British government later claimed it was justified in setting the fires because Americans had burned several government buildings in Toronto two years earlier. But at least one British officer thought the burning of Washington was a barbaric act. According to Major Harry Smith, "It made one ashamed to be an Englishman. We felt more like a band of savages from the woods."

Led by Cockburn, British troops entered the

Capitol. At that time the building consisted of two wings, the House and the Senate, which were connected by a temporary wooden hallway. The center section and the massive dome were yet to be built. Stories later were told that in the House section Admiral Cockburn climbed to the podium, called his troops to order, and presented a mocking motion: "Shall this edifice of Yankee democracy be set to the torch? All for it say, 'aye.'" "Aye!" shouted a chorus of British soldiers. With that, the hallway was set ablaze and soldiers spread flaming boards throughout the building. Soon black smoke and orange flames gushed out of the broken windows.

The British troops next trudged down Pennsylvania Avenue. Their dusty red jackets glowed eerily in the light cast by the flames that danced behind them. The men were not wild-eyed maniacs eager to set ablaze everything they saw. Instead they were disciplined soldiers who burned only those buildings their officers ordered them to burn.

Admiral Cockburn seemed particulary gleeful when he entered the White House. He was surprised to discover that President Madison and his party had not even bothered to lock the front door. Once inside, Cockburn grabbed a couple of souvenirs—an old hat belonging to the president and a cushion from Dolley Madison's chair. Some British soldiers claimed that he and his officers helped themselves to food and wine left on the dining room table by the First Lady. After Cockburn rummaged about the White House, he gave the order to pile up the furniture and set it on fire.

Outside the White House, units of redcoats, acting under orders, set fire to the Treasury Building. Three prominent houses near Pennsylvania Avenue also were torched. The officers believed that American snipers lurked in those houses. As the British lighted these fires, towers of flame leaped out of the naval yard that spread along the banks of the Potomac River. That fire was set by retreating American forces to keep stores of powder, cannons, and river gunboats out of enemy hands.

From the Virginia hills overlooking Washington, President Madison and his party gazed down upon the burning capital. In the darkness it looked as though most of the town were ablaze. Attorney General Rush, who spent the evening with the president, claimed that he saw "columns of flame and smoke ascending throughout the night. . . .The President's House and other public edifices were on fire, some burning slowly, others with bursts of flame and sparks mounting high up in the horizon. . . .If at intervals the dismal sight was lost to our view, we got it again from one hilltop or eminence where we paused to look at it."

A sudden thunderstorm prevented the fire from spreading into other Washington neighborhoods. Many Washingtonians hiding in the woods and cornfields outside the capital hailed the storm as a miracle delivered by God. Others felt that while the rain saved many houses it also added to the gloom of a defeated people.

President Madison spent a frustrating, sleepless night in a house outside the capital. His military men had failed to defend the city, but he knew the American people would ultimately blame him for the humiliating defeat. Historian Leonard P. White later wrote that the burning of Washington marked "probably the lowest point ever attained in the prestige of the Presidency."

In the soggy morning the British prepared to leave the beleaguered city. Their mission had been to raid the capital; they never had any plans to occupy it. Before he rode off, Admiral Cockburn had his men wreck the office of Washington's most prominent newspaper, the *National Intelligencer.* A story holds that Cockburn commanded his troops specifically to destroy every letter *C* on the typesetter's bench so the paper would be unable to print the name Cockburn. The redcoats also intended to blow up the United States Patent Office, but there they were stopped by the superintendent of patents, Dr. William Thornton. He told the British officer in charge of the demolition crew that the inventions and models housed inside would benefit all mankind. To their credit, the British spared the building.

After the last British soldier marched away,

Washingtonians streamed back into their city like ants returning to a crushed hill. One of those returnees was the prominent society woman, Margaret Bayard Smith, who a week earlier had written so confidently about the troops defending Washington. This time her letter said, "In the afternoon we rode to the city. We passed several dead horses. The poor Capitol Building! Nothing but its blackened walls remained. Four or five houses in the neighborhood were also in ruins....the President's House.... which when I last visited it, was so splendid...was now nothing but ashes."

Washingtonians immediately began the job of cleaning up their city, but a dark cloud of defeat remained over the capital. Then, about three weeks after the burning of Washington, a hastily written poem helped lift the people's spirits.

The British fleet next sailed to the port of Baltimore. On September 13, 1814, cannons roared as British warships opened fire on Fort McHenry, near Baltimore. The bombardment lasted all day and well into the night. Francis Scott Key, Georgetown lawyer, was a prisoner on one of the British ships. He nervously paced the deck, fearing that the undermanned fort would be forced to surrender under such frightening shelling. But as the sun inched into the morning sky, Key caught sight of the Americn flag still waving above the battered fort. At that instant, he realized that the American defenders had stood fast!

In a burst of patriotism, Key pulled an unfinished letter from his pocket and hurriedly wrote a poem on the back of it. Later, a Baltimore singer read the poem and put the words to music. The most famous song in American history was born. From the burning of Washington came the victory at Fort McHenry which inspired the song starting with the lines:

Oh say, can you see, by the dawn's early light,
What so proudly we hailed at the twilight's last gleaming?

About the Author

R. Conrad Stein was born and grew up in Chicago. He enlisted in the Marine Corps at the age of eighteen and served for three years. He then attended the University of Illinois where he received a Bachelor's degree in history. He later studied in Mexico, earning an advanced degree from the University of Guanajuato. Mr. Stein is the author of many other books, articles, and short stories written for young people.

Mr. Stein is married to Deborah Kent, who is also a writer of books for young readers.

About the Artist:

Richard Wahl, graduate of the Art Center College of Design in Los Angeles, has illustrated a number of magazine articles and booklets. He is a skilled artist and photographer who advocates realistic interpretations of his subjects. He lives with his wife and two sons in Louisville, Kentucky.